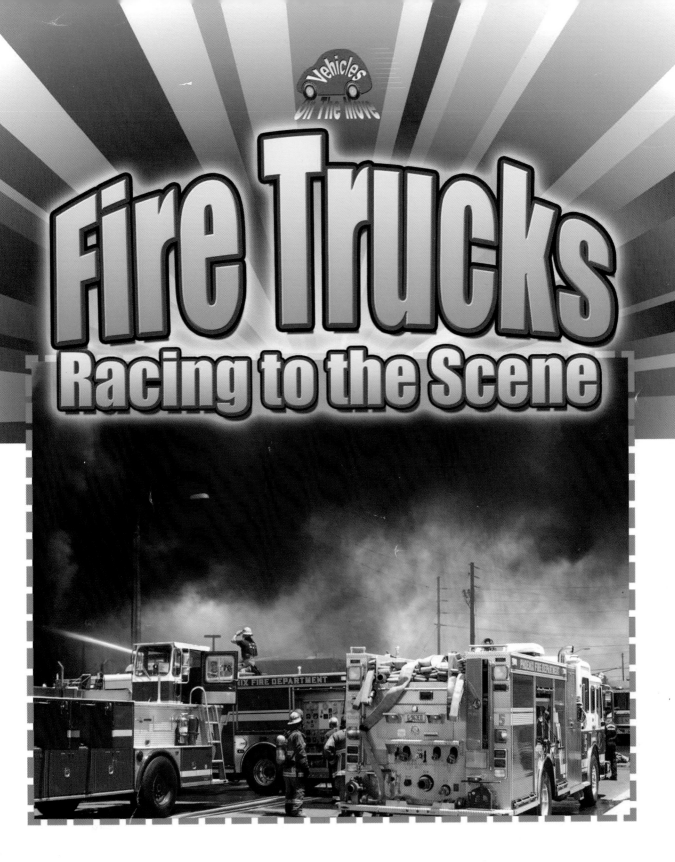

Vehicles On The Move

Fire Trucks
Racing to the Scene

Molly Aloian

Crabtree Publishing Company

www.crabtreebooks.com

Created by Bobbie Kalman

Author
Molly Aloian

Editorial director
Kathy Middleton

Project editor
Paul Challen

Editor
Adrianna Morganelli

Proofreaders
Rachel Stuckey
Reagan Miller

Photo research
Melissa McCLellan

Design
Tibor Choleva

Production coordinators
Katherine Berti
Margaret Amy Salter

Prepress technicians
Katherine Berti
Margaret Amy Salter

Consultant
Captain Ken Prine

Special thanks to
Sandor Monos

Illustrations
All illustrations by Leif Peng

Photographs
Dreamstime.com: © Robert Guildig (title page); © Olivier Le Queinec (table of contents page); © Jim Parkin (page 5); © Wally Stemberger (page 11); © Shane Link (page 16); © Robert Guildig (17 bottom); © Svlumagraphica (page 20–21); © Christopher Jensen (page 21 top); © Carlos Santa Maria (pages 22–23); © Paul Kazmercyk (page 24); © Tad Denson (page 28 inset); © Uladzimir Chaberkus (pages 28–29); © Jim Parkin (page 31)
Shutterstock.com: © mikeledray (front cover); © Losevsky Pavel (page 6–7); © Rob Wilson (page 8); © David Touchtone (page 9); © bbbb (page 12); © Monkey Business Images (13 top); © Lilac Mountain (13 bottom); © Donald R. Swartz (pages 14–15); © Brian McDonald (page 17 top); © Joy Brown (page 18); © Mike Brake (page 19); © daseaford (page 25 top); © TFoxFoto (page 25); © Peter Kim (page 26); © Denis Barbulat (page 30 top)
Istockphoto: © SabinaS (page 4); © slobo (page 10); © visualpeople (back cover, page 27)
Public Domain: page 30

Library and Archives Canada Cataloguing in Publication

Aloian, Molly
   Fire trucks : racing to the scene / Molly Aloian.

(Vehicles on the move)
Includes index.
Issued also in an electronic format.
ISBN 978-0-7787-3046-0 (bound).--ISBN 978-0-7787-3060-6 (pbk.)

   1. Fire engines--Juvenile literature. I. Title. II. Series: Vehicles on the move

TH9372.A46 2011   j628.9'259   C2010-904798-2

Library of Congress Cataloging-in-Publication Data

CIP available at Library of Congress

Crabtree Publishing Company

www.crabtreebooks.com   1-800-387-7650
Printed in the U.S.A./082010/BA20100709

Published in Canada
Crabtree Publishing
616 Welland Ave.
St. Catharines, ON
L2M 5V6

Published in the United States
Crabtree Publishing
PMB 59051
350 Fifth Avenue, 59th Floor
New York, New York 10118

Published in the United Kingdom
Crabtree Publishing
Maritime House
Basin Road North, Hove
BN41 1WR

Published in Australia
Crabtree Publishing
386 Mt. Alexander Rd.
Ascot Vale (Melbourne)
VIC 3032

Contents

Fire, fire! 4

Take a closer look 6

Why red? 8

Lights and sirens 10

Carrying tools 12

The pumper truck 14

Hooking up 16

The ladder truck 18

The tiller ladder truck 20

The quint truck 22

Rescue trucks 24

The tanker truck 26

The foam unit 28

A long time ago ... 30

Words to know and Index 32

Fire, fire!

A **fire truck** is a **vehicle**. Vehicles are machines that move from place to place. Fire trucks carry firefighters and equipment to the site of a fire. This picture shows a fire truck racing down a street to a fire.

Fire truck drivers must be careful to avoid accidents when racing to fires.

Different fire trucks

There are different types of fire trucks. All of them are huge! Some fire trucks carry water to a fire. Others carry tools that help rescue people from danger. If the fire is big, many fire trucks may be called.

This team of fire trucks is rushing to a scene of a big fire.

Take a closer look

Fire trucks do jobs that no other vehicle can. Different fire trucks have different parts. Each part does a different job. This fire truck is an elevated platform truck. It has a huge ladder with a platform at one end. Firefighters standing on the platform can reach the windows of tall buildings and rescue people.

ladder platform

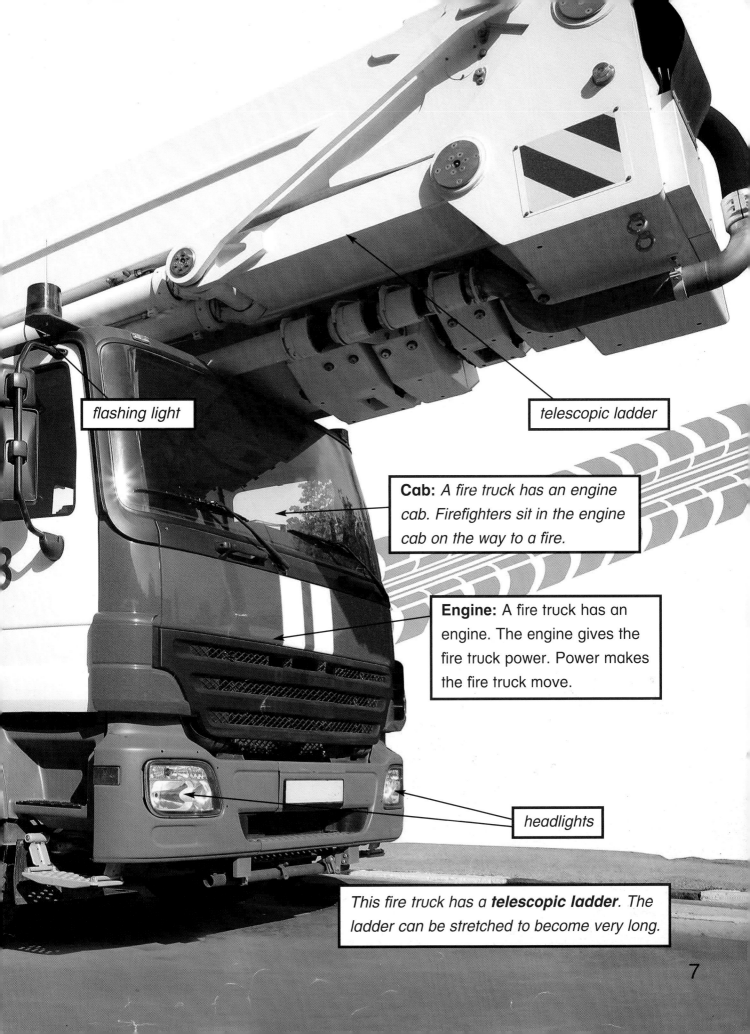

flashing light

telescopic ladder

Cab: *A fire truck has an engine cab. Firefighters sit in the engine cab on the way to a fire.*

Engine: A fire truck has an engine. The engine gives the fire truck power. Power makes the fire truck move.

headlights

*This fire truck has a **telescopic ladder**. The ladder can be stretched to become very long.*

Why red?

Hundreds of years ago, most of the cars that people drove were painted black. Fire trucks were painted red so they would stand out. Today, most fire trucks are red. Others are bright yellow, green, or white. These bright colors still help fire trucks get noticed on the road.

Most fire trucks are painted red.

Night light

In some smaller cities where there are fewer city lights and roads are dark at night, all the fire trucks are painted bright yellow. Bright yellow is easier for people to see at night. Some trucks have **reflective stripes**. Reflective strips glow in the dark. The strips make the trucks easier to see in the dark.

Fire trucks that are painted yellow stand out against the dark sky at night.

Lights and sirens

All fire trucks have lights and sirens. The lights are bright and the sirens are very loud. The lights and sirens are turned on as the firefighters race to a fire. The lights and sirens let people know that firefighters are on their way!

Flashing lights and loud sirens warn people and other vehicles on the roads that speeding fire trucks are coming by.

Move out of the way!

The lights and sirens on a fire truck warn other drivers on the road to pull over and make room for the fire truck to get through. Fire trucks must get to the fires as quickly as possible so they can put out the fire and help people who are in danger.

stopped traffic

speeding fire truck

reflective stripe

Cars on the road have to stop and let fire trucks pass by safely.

Carrying tools

All fire trucks have storage compartments for carrying tools and equipment. Firefighters need special tools and equipment to fight fires. Helmets, goggles, and axes are examples of some of the tools firefighters need.

air tanks

fuel tank

chain saws

fire extinguishers

power generator

digging and prying tools

Fire trucks also carry first-aid supplies, such as rubber gloves, scissors, and bandages. Firefighters use these supplies to help people who are hurt at the scene of a fire. The firefighter in this picture is also a paramedic.

ladders

helmet

This firefighter is wearing a **self-contained breathing apparatus**. *It helps the firefighter breathe in places filled with smoke.*

radio

gloves

pump controls

fire-resistant clothing

reflective stripes

Firefighters rescue animals trapped in fires, too. This firefighter is carrying a cat rescued from a burning house.

13

The pumper truck

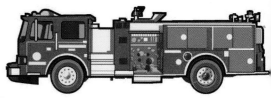

The pumper truck is usually the first truck to arrive at the scene of a fire. The pumper truck carries long **hoses**. It also carries tools such as axes, saws, and flashlights, which firefighters need to break down walls or pry open doors that are stuck or locked.

lights

engine

cab

siren

EMS

ENGINE NO. 3

FIRE DEPT.

14

Blasting water

There are strong pumps inside the pumper truck. The pumps blast water out of the hoses with great force. A pumper truck can pump over 1,000 gallons (3,785 liters) of water in just one minute. The water blasts out very hard!

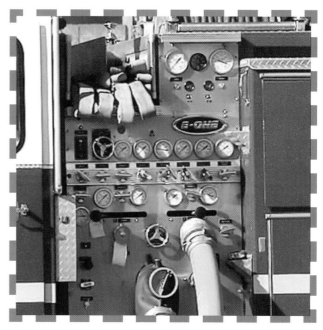

The pumper truck's pump panel is used to control the strength of the water blast.

water blast

pump panel

storage compartments

hose

Hooking up

At the scene of a fire, a pumper truck needs to find the nearest **fire hydrant**. A fire hydrant is a covered pipe that sticks out of the ground. It is connected to a water supply that is underground. The firefighters connect the pumper truck's hose to the fire hydrant.

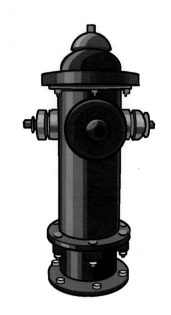

This firefighter is connecting a fire truck hose to a fire hydrant. A fire hydrant is like a big "tap."

Pumping water

The pumper truck then pumps the water from the fire hydrant into other hoses that are also connected to the pumper truck. Firefighters carry these hoses to the fire and spray water onto the flames until the fire is out.

Firefighters must be strong to be able to hold the hose and aim it toward the fire.

Pumper trucks have powerful pumps. They can spray water over long distances.

The ladder truck

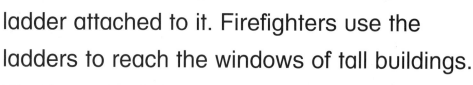

A **ladder truck** is a fire truck that has a huge ladder attached to it. Firefighters use the ladders to reach the windows of tall buildings. The bottom of the ladder is on a **turntable**. A turntable is a platform that turns. The ladder on a ladder truck can turn in any direction.

This firefighter is climbing up the ladder to spray water on the burning roof.

water pipe

firefighter operating a turntable

Rise up

The driver of the ladder truck uses controls to turn the ladder toward the fire. He or she also uses the controls to raise the ladder. Most ladder trucks have water pipes built onto the ladder. Water gushes through those pipes toward the fire.

The tiller ladder truck

A tiller ladder truck is a long fire truck. It has ladders that can extend, or stretch, like a telescope. These ladders can extend very high—over 100 feet (30 meters) into the air.

Two is better than one

A tiller truck has two steering wheels—one at the back of the truck and one at the front. One driver steers the front of the truck. A second driver steers the back of the truck. The drivers talk to each other on a radio about where they want to move the truck.

back steering wheel

ladder

HOOK &

FAST PAK

FIRE

Firefighters can climb up the ladder and fight roof fires safely.

front steering wheel

The quint truck

A quint truck is both a pumper truck and a ladder truck. The word "quint" comes from the Latin word for "five." This truck can do five different jobs. It has a pump, a water tank, a hose, and two kinds of ladders. It has ground ladders as well as an aerial ladder.

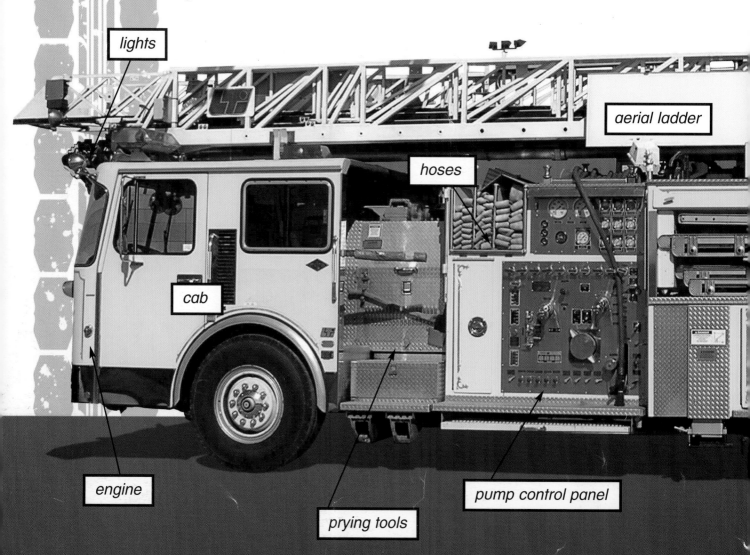

lights

aerial ladder

hoses

cab

engine

prying tools

pump control panel

All in one

The quint truck has the tools and equipment of both the pumper truck and the ladder truck. This way, firefighters have everything they may need on one truck.

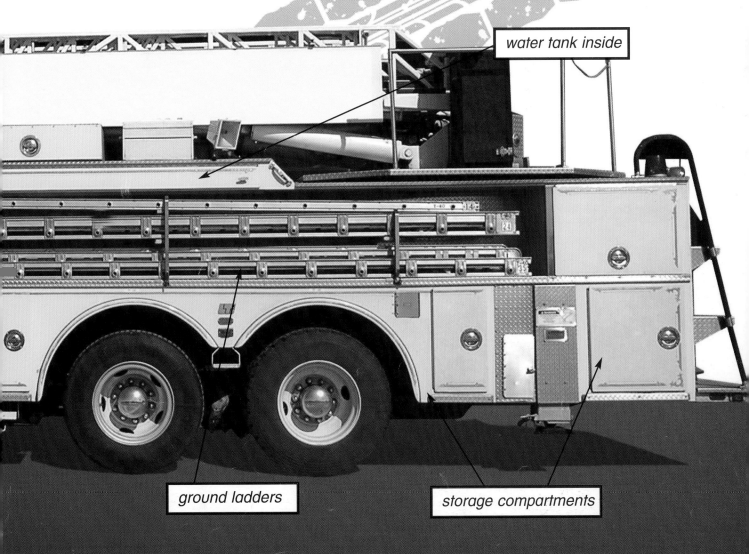

water tank inside

ground ladders

storage compartments

Rescue trucks

Some fire trucks carry tools and equipment to help rescue people who are trapped in cars after car accidents.

Rescue trucks have compartments where all tools and equipment are stored.

Power!

During floods, earthquakes, tornadoes, or other disasters, there may be no electricity to power lights or electric tools. Some rescue trucks can create their own electricity. Electricity is very important during an emergency!

Fire trucks carry power generators so that they can create their own electricity.

This firefighter is using the "Jaws of Life" to rescue a person from a crushed vehicle. This tool is like a pair of scissors, but it is much more powerful. It can cut through thick metal.

The tanker truck

A **tanker truck** is a large fire truck with a huge tank that is filled with water. It carries water to the scene of a fire and the firefighters use the water to put out the fire.

FIRE-RESCUE

WT89

water tank

Fires can start in fields or forests, too. Tanker trucks carry water to fight fires in places where there are no fire hydrants.

Filled with water

The tanker truck is useful in small villages or towns where there may not be a fire hydrant close to a fire. Most tanker trucks carry 1,000 gallons (3,785 liters) of water. But there are some tanker trucks that can carry up to 5,000 gallons (18,927 liters) of water!

Some tanker trucks are painted white. This tanker truck was used to carry water to the site of a forest fire.

The foam unit

Some tanker trucks are called **foam units**. They carry a special type of foam as well as water. Foam units can put out fires that cannot be put out with just water. These fires are called flammable liquid fires. Gasoline is a flammable liquid. Putting out a gasoline fire can be very dangerous.

These airport foam unit trucks are speeding toward a fire at an airport.

Spray foam

A foam unit can carry up to 3,434 gallons (13,000 liters) of water and up to 264 gallons (1,000 liters) of foam. It can pump over 793 gallons (3,000 liters) of water or 594 gallons (2,250 liters) of foam in just one minute!

A long time ago...

Long ago, there were no fire trucks. When there was a fire, people had to carry buckets of water by hand. This was called a **bucket brigade**. The first fire trucks with pumps needed as many as 28 people to work the pumps!

This picture shows a fire truck from long ago.

Many people were needed to fight fires before modern fire trucks were invented.

Big changes

In 1852, the steam-powered fire truck was invented. The engine was called Uncle Joe Ross. It was named after a politician in Cincinnati who helped get the truck built. In time, people built gasoline-powered fire trucks that could carry hoses, tools, and gear. Fire trucks have changed a lot over the years, but all of them still race to the scene of a fire!

This steam pumper truck was built in 1889. It is being towed to a fire truck fair.

Words to know and Index

fire hydrant
pages 16, 17, 26, 27

hose
pages 14, 15, 16, 17

ladder truck
pages 18–19

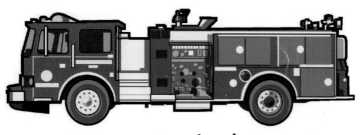

pumper truck
pages 14–15

rescue truck
pages 24-25

Other index words

aerial ladder 22
bucket brigade 30
engine 7, 14, 22, 31
foam unit 28–29
quint truck 22–23
tiller ladder truck 20–21
turntable 18, 19

tanker truck
pages 26–27